THE ENERGY SHIFT

The Energy Shift

Increase Your Energy and Do More of What You Want Every Day

Copyright c 2016 by Ritu Rao | Rao Media
Ritu Rao
Rao Media
P. O. Box 742903
Dallas, Texas 75374

ISBN 13: 978-0-9965141-1-8
ISBN-10: 0-9965141-1-2

Printed in the United States of America

10 9 8 7 6 5 4 3 2 1

THE ENERGY SHIFT

Increase Your Energy and
Do More of What You Want Every Day

RITU RAO

Table of Contents

To each little step that takes you closer.

How to Get the Most Out of This Book

AT FIRST, I wrote this book for me. I wanted to feel more often like I was living rather than just existing, and I wanted to increase the energy level in my life. Then I thought, surely I'm not the only one who could benefit from these improvements, so I decided to share what I'd learned.

I wanted to look beyond the 'eat better, get more exercise' options, although I strongly believe that a foundation of good health is necessary to grow personally or professionally in any area.

Growth takes work, and I want my work to count. With this in mind, I aim to build habits and systems rather than rely on the latest trend, quick results, or my willpower, which has all too often proven fickle. I have found that small shifts in perspective and action can, when combined and done consistently, produce significant change that enhances the quality of life.

The energy I'm attracted to and therefore strive to cultivate is not the loud, frenetic, or boisterous kind. Rather, it is the calm, positive, strong and steady force—an aura, so to speak—which I find greatly appealing. When a person with this kind of energy enters my life, I gravitate toward him or her. This type of person tends to have a confident air, is often successful, has rich life experiences, and displays interesting personality traits. This isn't the kind of energy you get from your fourth cup of coffee. This energy goes deeper, transcending all aspects of life, and gives a sense of vitality that is less common than I wish it were.

So I started to dig, and in this book I share what I found: what, how, and why it works for me as long as I practice it. To get the most out of this, or any book, I recommend this approach:

➤ If you're reading purely for entertainment, read the book once and you're done.

➤ If you want to learn something, highlight and make notes.

➤ If you want it to stick, re-read the book and your notes every so often.

➤ If you truly want a change in your life, re-read and apply what you've learned, one or two small things at a time, on a regular basis.

Since one size doesn't fit all, take from this book whatever works for you to find your own way, and shift forward.

I don't know where I'm going from here, but I promise it won't be boring.

~ David Bowie

Making The Cut

I LOOKED DOWN at my watch in the pitch dark, and the number 43 glowed under the light of my headlamp. Seven more miles to go; to run, walk, or crawl past the finish line.

The sun had set a long time ago, and I willed myself to keep going. I kept clasping my freezing hands to shake off the numbness, regretting my decision to forgo an extra shirt. I tried not to focus on that. I also tried not to focus on how much my body hurt, on how almost everyone else was done with this race hours ago, on how slowly I was moving. I was in the middle of the woods, but I couldn't quit so close to the end. Seven. More. Miles.

It seemed like forever, and by most runners' standards, it was. But my only goal was to finish. This was the longest race I'd ever attempted, and barring serious injury or illness, I had no reason to quit. When you toss talent and speed out of the picture, persistence is all you have left.

As I neared the last aid station, I started to worry. The last thing I wanted was to keep running, but it'd be far worse if I had to stop because I missed the cutoff time. I slowed my shuffle, and a volunteer came rushing, asking me if I needed anything, if I was all right. "Do I have time? Can I finish?" I asked. "You're good," he said, "only a couple of more miles. Take it home."

I didn't even stop. If I did, it'd be even harder to start again. I had started this race fourteen hours ago, and I was going to finish it. You'd think the distance would be more intimidating at the start, but those last couple of miles felt the longest, the toughest, the most grueling.

I finally made it, just eleven minutes shy of the cutoff. I didn't even have the decency to be last and win the DFL (dead fucking last) prize. But I made it—I completed my first-ever 50-mile trail race.

Fully Alive

In his book, *What I Talk About When I Talk About Running*, author Haruki Murakami says, "if you're going to while away the years, it's far better to live them with clear goals and fully alive than in a fog."

My views have shifted away from keeping goals, but the two words that caught my attention were "fully alive," because I wanted to shift my life in that direction. Those words don't mean to me today what they did just a few years ago. Before, they were a platitude: unrelatable, feel-good, forgettable words. Now, they are a guide of sorts, a check-in point for most decisions, and much less scary than their alternative.

Engaging in a physical challenge is one way to feel alive. I chose a challenge for myself, and I'm sure many would concur that physical challenges deliver quite well in terms of feeling alive. But there are ways to feel alive that need not be occasional, nor so tremendous, and do not require numbness.

Where Do You Live?

Each day you wake up, you have two choices: live the day or drag through it. I'm going to guess you're here because you prefer the first option. And I don't mean living in the basic sense of heart still working, lungs still breathing; I mean living in the sense of feeling alert, vital, vibrant.

To do that, you need energy. What's that? According to *Webster's New Collegiate Dictionary* (entry trimmed with adjustments):

en-er-gy: 1: the capacity of acting or being active. 2: natural power vigorously executed. 3. the capacity for doing work.

Distilled to its essence: Energy = Strength + Vitality.

We usually think of energy in terms of the first part of that equation. But energy is more than just the vehicle to cross off our to-do list, or that frantic, caffeine-induced high during which we expect miraculous results. Optimizing your personal energy, the kind that is focused, calm, and useful for the long term, can allow you to do more of what matters to you, which then makes life more fulfilling and meaningful. It's the difference between surviving ("I'm so glad this day is done with") and thriving ("It was a tough day, but I made it").

You need energy to get things done. You also need energy to maintain good health, solve problems, conquer challenges, create, persist, play, have fun, give to others, expand, and live a bigger life. If any of those matter to you, you're going to need energy to make them happen, and sustain them over time.

The good news here is that while spent time is gone forever, energy is a (relatively) renewable resource. I see it as an asset you can develop and optimize within this limited time, setting you up for the best chances to succeed.

None of us are getting out alive, but it's up to us to decide how alive we want to feel while we're here.

Filling Your Needs

Beyond daily tasks, energy impacts every vital area of your life: personal health, relationships, friendships, children, work, hopes and dreams, level of success, enthusiasm, even your general attitude towards the world and yourself.

That's a long list.

In our desire to be more successful or productive, we tend to focus more on our attempts to increase or manage time and less on managing or increasing energy. Not that time isn't important, but what good is more time if you don't have the energy to use it?

Let's say I wave a magic wand and grant you an extra two hours every day. Would you have the energy to do what you want with that time? A 26-hour day sounds great, but not so much if you're exhausted by hour 10.

With better energy, you can get more done than what you're doing now, or do it more efficiently, with better focus and within the 24 hours you already have (sorry, no magic wand).

Years ago, I had no idea about the concept of personal energy, let alone how to consider changing it. In my mind, you were how you were, and if you were gifted a better set of genes, you were one of the lucky ones and got more than the rest.

What changed my mind—and eventually my life—was utter exhaustion; mental, physical, and emotional. It was a time when all looked good on paper, but inside I felt frustrated, unhappy, and defeated. I was stressed and stuck in my business, overwhelmed and sleep-deprived with a toddler and an infant, and try as I might, I couldn't figure out what I'd done wrong to end up feeling that low and without a choice. I'm sure the sleep deprivation had a lot to do with it, but even in my haze I knew that wasn't the entire picture.

A particular moment from that time remains vivid in my memory. In that moment, around 3 or 4 AM one sluggish morning, I realized three things:

> ➤ My exhaustion was a cumulative result of several choices.

> ➤ If I didn't start making some changes, things would most likely continue down this path.

> ➤ If I wanted something to change, I would have to be the one to do it.

Few moments in my life have been that clear and insightful. And because they are so rare, I knew I had to take this one seriously.

Slowly but surely, I put small changes into motion. Even slower still, my life began to shift. The possibility of change felt liberating, and watching it unfold after feeling trapped for the past few years was enough incentive to keep going. It was a welcome change from waiting, hoping, and wishing while feeling miserable. I was amazed yet baffled; why had no one told me about this?

It may sound silly, but even to this day I mentally refer to my life as 'before that day' and 'since that day' with regard to that 3 or 4 AM moment, as if it were a divider on my life's timeline. That's how different things seem before and after.

At this point, you might question whether things will turn around for you just because they did for me. They might not, or not as dramatically. This approach does not always produce sudden, dramatic results, because it is based upon a number of small shifts, which take time to implement as habits. However, I contend that by taking steps to better manage your personal energy, those small shifts will add up to a big difference, and you'll find your life turning around as well.

If the idea of turning small successes into bigger ones interests you or makes you feel alive, let's keep going.

Getting In The Flow

The concept of energy conjures different images for different people. The type of energy that matters to me, and most likely to you, is personal energy. Broadly, this includes:

> - physical energy to sustain basic body functions, maintain health, perform everyday tasks, and undertake physical activities involving fitness, sports, or endurance

> - creative mental energy for thinking, problem solving, developing ideas and concepts, imagination

> - energy related to self (thoughts, feelings, emotions, beliefs) and other people (relationships), responding/reacting to your environment

Each type of energy is in a different state of flow at a given time. Your energy state will be different in the morning after a night of good rest than, let's say, at the end of a tough day at work. It will not be the same while connecting with your best friend as it would be during a tough meeting with your boss.

In light of everyday events we typically face, most things that affect your energy state are energy drainers or energy fillers.

Energy Drainers: anything or anyone that triggers a drop in your energy, or a net negative effect. These include health issues, toxic people (those in whose presence you feel badly about yourself), stressors (conflicts, fears, not meeting expectations, unfulfilling habits), negative thinking patterns, a negative environment.

Energy Fillers: anything or anyone that triggers an increase in your energy, or a net positive effect. These include healthy habits/lifestyles, being around people who are loving and supporting, relaxers (up-lifting events such as pursuing interests, hobbies, creative endeavors, activities that encourage growth and learning), positive thinking patterns, a positive environment.

By referring to the above factors as positive or negative, I'm referring to how we generally perceive them, respond to them, and whether they bring us down or lift us up. To maximize personal energy, it follows that you would need to maximize the fillers and minimize the drainers.

If only life were that black and white. While perfection is an unrealistic expectation, we each have the capacity to tip the scale in favor of fillers by making small changes, or shifts. Rumi said, "As you start to walk out on the way, the way appears." Shifts add up over time, and even if you don't know exactly where they will lead, small efforts almost always compound into big impact.

Powering Up

If your personal energy is lower than you want it to be, I recommend starting by taking a look at the basics: diet, exercise, sleep, hydration, and stress level. I'm not a fitness expert, but fitness can always begin with straightforward common sense. I found it the simplest place to begin putting small changes into motion, which was good because simple was all I could handle at the time. I knew I had to work on my physical health first, because it's impossible to think clearly when you're always exhausted.

My simple choices were: more moving, better eating, more sleeping, and more delegating to my husband (no more of "I need to do it all" if help was available). I decided it was time to work on losing the extra thirty pounds I had adopted.

Later in the week of my "big moment," I joined a gym. I began a basic running program. I didn't know it then, but running was going to change my life.

Looking back, that was when I started to become more conscious and aware. It makes such a difference. Being at the gym felt new and serious, the act of someone who meant business. It was also awkward and uncomfortable, especially when most people around me already seemed in shape, but I cranked up my music and stuck to my plan. It felt good to be doing something, even if it was just for 20 minutes.

Slowly, things started to come together. The fog began to lift, the extra pounds started to come off; I felt more hopeful and less stuck. The high of seeing progress kept me going from one day to the next. Even at work, I took small steps, and made decisions where I had procrastinated. Things were still tough, and there were times when I saw no results, but the overall trend was improvement. I clung to that. Funny how one can read about this stuff a gazillion times, but only when it clicks does the message hit home.

It was clear to me that:

→Energy affects your mood, your output, and your outlook. It seriously impacts your relationships and decision-making.

→Be energy-rich, and you think more clearly. Be energy-poor, and you sink deeper into the fog and away from the life you want to live.

And if the choice is between rich or poor, you'd pick rich, right? But like any lasting, worthwhile change, rich takes work. Many people harbor the illusion that they are stuck with what they've got. My purpose in writing this book is to poke giant holes in that illusion, and then to help make the work of optimizing your energy more doable.

In the following chapters, I break down each major component that impacts your energy and offer suggestions for shifts you can incorporate into your life. These small changes will add up, giving you a reliable system you can use (yet modify when needed) to do more of what you want, faster and better, in your career, relationships, and personal life.

Let's get started.

1

Mindset

Most of us have two lives: the life we live, and the unlived life within us.
~ Steven Pressfield, Author

I ONCE READ that we humans are so invested in making the "right" decision that even if we find we don't like the path we have chosen, we hang in there for dear life.

That's how much we resist change. We do not like it.

I found myself reading that a few times, to let the meaning sink in, and because I like to be right as often as I can (okay, always). The sentiment's original author, Dr. Susan Jeffers, continued on to make a good point: if something is not "right" anymore, there is value in learning that it isn't. There's even more value in knowing it's time for change.

But we don't like change, remember? Especially if we have to be the ones to do it.

This may be where you feel your first unease. If so, that's quite natural. But I've noticed that if we want more, better, different, or anywhere-but-here, something will need to change. Change reduces the disconnect between where we are and where we want to be. And because we resist change even if we say we want it, we need a real reason to make that shift.

Real reasons are different from easy reasons, which are the excuses we settle into just like our favorite and familiar chair in the living room. If you want more energy, what's your real reason?

Is it so you can get more done in a day? To keep up with your kids? To grow your business and help it succeed? Perhaps, with more energy, you can finally pursue that dream, the one you've been putting off for "someday." Sometimes it's as simple as being tired of being tired. Or maybe you want all in. Perhaps days blurring into one another is not on your life's plan. Rather than be a passive spectator, watching the world pass you by, you want to live, darn it! You want a more conscious life, full of vitality and enthusiasm.

Okay! But it's not always easy figuring out why. You might start with your dissatisfaction (the easy reason), working your way to what is important to you (the real reason). Two words: dig deep.

What makes you feel tapped out and scraping the bottom of your energy barrel? Take a step back from your immediate frustrations and examine those problems. Keep stepping back till you see the bigger picture or familiar patterns. You might notice that your reason goes beyond finishing that next big project or avoiding the daily three o'clock crash. My biggest block was frequently feeling tired and low and thinking "this is normal."

When you distill down your real reason (remember: dig deeeep), it will help you move beyond simply wishing and into consciously deciding. I love to make wishes and send them up into the air, just in case, but when I decide to do something, things tend to happen and time is again my friend.

TRY THIS SHIFT

Grab some good ol' fashioned pen and paper. Ask yourself the following questions:

1) What is the most 'tiring point' in my life right now? What am I missing out on? Examples:

> ➤ I'm too tired to hang out with my kids every day.

> ➤ I feel drained at work by 3 pm.

> ➤ I don't have the energy or the time to exercise...ever.

> ➤ I'm often in a low mood.

2) If I don't change anything, what will happen? How will I feel a week, a month, a year from now?

3) If I do change something, what will happen? How will I feel a week, a month, a year from now?

This process has the effect of leading your thinking, and therefore your mindset, beyond your current frustration to the deeper desires you're trying to ful-fill. By starting with your mindset, you're setting the stage and considering a story different than the one you've been telling yourself; the easy reasons, the excuses. And because change brings out an instinctive resistance for so many, the story you want to live is going to need this mindset, or it will be too easy to let go unfinished.

In his book, *A Million Miles in A Thousand Years*, Donald Miller writes:

> Here's the truth about telling stories with your life. It's going to sound like a great idea, and you are going to get excited about it, and then when it comes time to do the work, you're not going to do it. It's like that with writing books, and it's like that with life. People love to have lived a great story, but few people like the work it takes to make it happen.

If you want more energy–if you want things to be different–decide that they must be, and let that changed mindset lead the charge.

BENEFITS

> ➢ Leading questions probe deeper than current frustrations.

> ➢ Deeper probing helps clarify real desires.

> ➢ Writing them down helps articulate your thoughts more clearly.

➢ As with anything worth having long term, getting the right mindset is key because it helps you stay centered when the inevitable obstacles arise.

2

Pushing the Right Buttons: Food

It is much easier to follow a script than to develop the awareness and flexibility to be your own person.
~ Daniele Bolelli, Writer, Professor, Martial Artist

MORE THAN ONCE, I've found myself staring at my computer after it decided to turn against me. A frozen screen, new tabs that don't open, save function that doesn't cooperate, those sorts of things. When my impressive collection of swear words doesn't persuade the computer to cooperate, I typically embark on lots of clicking, which gets more random and vigorous as the problem grows worse. Hell hath no fury like a woman scorning her non-compliant laptop. Parts of this scenario might sound familiar to you.

In my frustration, I'm usually on page 4 of a Google search before I remember to try something basic: turn the computer off, then back on. There it was, a simple solution, one which works most of the time, and was always available to me. But in my frustration, I ignored the simple possibility and went on to search for something more complex.

This is how we tend to be. When facing an immediate problem—let's say, a lack of energy—we often forget to check the basics first.

Your diet is the first of those basics. It's the thing that fuels you, so it's the first button to push. The relationship looks like this:

Better fuel → better health → more energy.

Easy to say, but looks daunting to do, right? Between the food industry, expectations on our time, our lifestyles and our habits, maintaining a healthy diet resembles an obstacle course. Our mission is to navigate that course as best we can. And for that, there's good news and bad news.

The bad news: the path to healthy eating has many detours, some of which lead the wrong way, and some are too hard to travel without sacrificing convenience and sanity.

The good news: the resources available today can provide helpful navigation beacons. And like most newnesses, once you get through the initial phase, things aren't as difficult as you had imagined.

One of the greatest blocks is the impulse to figure out the whole method before starting, the impulse to make no changes until you figure out whether to go Paleo, or plant-based, or on Name Brand shakes. The idea of small shifts seems unworthy of consideration. Here again, it is better to do small things than get bound up seeking a Grand Plan and end up taking no action at all.

Most of healthy eating applies common sense to basic knowledge: less processed food, more whole foods, more plants, more fiber, smaller portions. I recommend testing what works for you along those lines, taking some notes, and thus compiling a guide from experience applied to common sense and your breadth of basic knowledge. This is a great and valuable starting point.

Here's something about most of us: when how we eat makes us feel negative, we register that association. But when our eating makes us feel positive and energetic, we don't note that nearly as often. That's unfortunate, because it is just as important to increase positive feeling as it is to reduce negative feelings.

For example, you've probably experienced an energy crash after loading up on sugar, or that bloated feeling after a heavy meal. How often have you experimented with a week or two of healthy eating while making note of your mood, your decision-making ability, your energy level? Probably not ever.

Why is this? I believe that we tend to attribute our mood and energy levels to events going on in our lives, and don't consider our diet to be a factor unless there's an obvious and immediate (negative) effect. My point is that if less-than-ideal food choices can sap our energy, closer-to-ideal food choices can keep our batteries charged.

In my own world, serious running training made me begin to pay more attention to what I ate. As I increased the distance, fuel became more important, and not just during my marathons and ultramarathons. Once the awareness kicked in, it spilled over to the rest of my life, and has stayed even when I'm not training.

The change was neither automatic nor overnight. Once I was aware of how my food choices affected my performance, it took conscious effort to train myself to eat better. But the interesting part is that even after an occasional indulgence or two, I noticed the list of tempting unhealthy foods shrinking over time. This led to more experimentation with the healthy foods that I liked, to make them more appetizing. I have noticed a definite change in my tastes, which are different than even a few short years ago. But you don't need to participate in a sport as an incentive to stay in shape. You could have other incentives, such as a desire to control weight, cut down on your medications, or have more energy to keep up with your kids.

When faced with a food choice I might struggle with, I find what helps me is a mix of responses:

➤ Mindset: strong desire (I want to stay healthy)

➤ Will power: supremely unreliable on a regular basis unless you've trained for it, but occasionally effective ("I don't need to eat this")

➤ The quality of questions I ask myself: not "should I eat this," but "do I really want to put this in my body?"

➤ The desire to avoid a negative consequence: "I don't want to break my good streak for today/this week," imagining how sluggish my next workout will be. Or my big one: I don't want to go on any medications.

There are times these responses don't work for me, but they are rare. It's not a perfect plan, but rather part of a system I rely on, and I'd rather have an imperfect system than none at all.

A special note on caffeine:

Bet you were wondering when this would come up. We're talking about energy, after all. More caffeine, more energy, right?

Not exactly.

I'm not anti-caffeine. I happen to love my daily cup or two of coffee, and tea every so often. I also happen to love the caffeine kick that gets my day going. But it would be silly to put all my energy eggs into one caffeinated basket.

Caffeine hits are temporary fixes. I have found it important not to confuse a temporary fix with a long-term, fully functional system. Both are useful, but you have to know when to use each. Caffeine can be part of my energy system, but can't be my entire system.

TRY THIS SHIFT

I can't tell you what to eat, nor can anyone else, because no one knows what diet is 100% right for you. This is proven by the fact that a hot new diet emerges practically every day, backed by fractional scientific evidence, and promises miracles. The confusion alone can stop you in your tracks, or derail the best intentions. To that end I propose the 'common sense' guide, which is less trendy but always available, and has a steady if unglamorous track record. In the simplest of terms:

Eat less junk, eat more whole/real foods.

That may sound vague, but it represents the core of most diets. Most diets agree on choosing reasonable portions while decreasing processed foods, excess sugar/salt, fried foods, and other components known to be less healthy. Start there. I can only give you general guidance because food choices are so personal and emotional that only you can steer your ship.

After you improve the basic quality of what you eat, you can tackle the common pitfalls that lead most of us to poorer food choices, and act in the way that solves each one:

➤ Temptation: if you don't buy it, you're less likely to eat it.

➤ Inconvenience: make the good stuff more handy and keep it within reach. If you're in a rush, you're more likely to grab what's closest.

➤ Laziness: pick simple, easy recipes, then rotate them. No need to try a hundred new things at once.

➤ Bland, unappetizing food: there are a host of quick, easy, inexpensive resources at your disposal. The options are not as limited as they might seem. There are better cooking techniques, better ways to season food, and go-to cookbooks that specialize in fast, tasty, healthy eating.

> ➢ Lack of planning: a little bit goes a long way. A few extra minutes of prepping, freezing leftovers, or using the same ingredients in different ways can make a significant difference.

> ➢ Forgetting the other basics: I'll discuss these in more detail in later chapters, but underestimating the importance of sleep, stress, and exercise will dent the results an improved diet can deliver. Taking care of the other basics is necessary for optimum results.

Every single food choice toward better eating is a small shift; do it consistently and the habit builds, the cravings recede, and the I-feel-good moments add up.

BENEFITS

> ➢ Better quality fuel in → more energy out.

> ➢ Approaching what you eat as a whole lays a better foundation not just for your energy level, but your overall health.

> ➢ What you eat as part of your lifestyle is a lot less stressful than a trendy diet, and the effects last longer.

> ➢ This shift also reduces reliance on caffeine and willpower, and maintains consistently higher energy levels.

3

Pushing the Right Buttons: Sleep

It is easier to resist at the beginning than at the end.
~ Leonardo da Vinci, Inventor, Painter

IT IS A truth universally acknowledged that the lower the battery power on your iPhone, the faster your panic level rises. Your eyes suddenly gain laser focus scanning for outlets, while your hands grasp for that magical white cord to complete the connection. When red turns to green, all hail the glory that is good.

Odd how we are less cognizant of the power of our bodies than that of our phones, and more nonchalant about the need to recharge bodies than the phones.

If you are a Type A, OCD, high achiever personality (or whatever label you prefer), you might already be on your way to dismissing this whole sleep thing. It was a constant interruption to play in toddlerhood, and now it's an inconvenience in adulthood. Sleeping less has become a badge of honor, an homage to the always-busy mindset.

Yet sleep is as miraculous as it is unsexy. Some crave it and are denied, whether due to health issues, crazy travel or work schedules, or resistant toddlers. The rest of us don't have much of an excuse–and still we underrate sleep, making it less of a priority than our devices and distractions. For some, it's emotional. In an interview, I heard a corporate manager speak about working long hours every day at an unfulfilling job, and coming home unhappy, mentally and physically drained. But sleep was the last thing on his mind. Instead, he chose to stay up late, drinking, watching TV, or going out. In his mind, going to bed early meant "they" won.

I've had the pleasure of placing sleep lower on the list of priorities, thanks to infants who liked to mix up their days and nights. Trust me, at 3 AM they are not as cute.

Aside from causing you to drag through your days, sleep deprivation inflicts mental and emotional side effects. In this lowered energy state, daily decisions feel more stressful, and tempers flare more easily. Your focus and your posture slip. You substitute coffee for sleep, and they aren't equivalent. I came to understand this sensation for longer than I enjoy remembering.

If you want the look and feel of success, this is hardly a scenario one would choose. When you walk into a meeting, an interview, or any situation where you dress to impress, you'd want to look and feel sharp, present, and attentive.

TRY THIS SHIFT

Plan to add 30 more minutes to your daily sleep time. Barring life changes, most of us are losing sleep for much less noble reasons. We're watching TV, or surfing the web, or shutting the laptop down with the intention to sleep early–then getting into bed to use the phone. Admit it: this isn't quality time, and none of the activities are urgent.

I recommend making it a plan, because without one, it probably won't happen. If setting an intention doesn't work, use a bedtime alarm and follow it. Trust me, Facebook will still be there tomorrow.

BENEFITS

➤ Rest and restoration to tackle each day.

➤ Improved immune and brain function.

➤ Healthier skin, weight control (the longer you stay awake, the more prone you are to late night snacking).

➤ A rested body and brain that can accomplish tasks faster and more efficiently.

➤ An energy reserve that helps you endure work or life challenges when you need to sacrifice sleep yet be in top form.

4

Pushing the Right Buttons:
Exercise

It can have meaning if it changes you for the better.
~ Viktor Frankl, Psychiatrist, Holocaust survivor

IF YOU JUST groaned, I understand. I usually have that reaction when I'm looking for a shorter, sexier solution, while ignoring the old-hat, less glamorous answer staring me in the face.

Try as we might, there's no escaping the biology of the human body. And try we do. Real food and sleep will take our energy levels far, but moving our body is an inevitable part of that equation. Movement optimizes it for better performance and sustained energy.

The word 'exercise' alone has become so emotionally charged. As the darling catchphrase for matters relating to weight loss, it has eclipsed the essence behind the shedding of pounds: movement, that thing our bodies are naturally meant to do. Our modern habits have compartmentalized movement into specific times and places, rather than making it a seamless part of our days.

I think it's time to change that.

To do so, put aside for a moment what exercise means to you personally, or what the media avalanche says, and focus on its basic purpose: to maintain bodily health and efficiency.

Important, right?

As a former expert in agreeing how good exercise is, then doing nothing about it, I am confident that I would have kept on that way had my energy not dipped so low. I got sick and tired of being tired, which got me to start moving. After that came the challenge of making the time to do it regularly, so I know it's not always easy. Life happens.

So the next time your best defense against exercise is that you're too tired, remember two things:

1. Exercise is precisely the way to build resistance to fatigue and boost your energy level, not only during exercise but long after you're done.

2. If I can go from a couch potato to an ultra-runner, practically anyone can become more active, including you.

Energy is what we need to fuel our engine so we can do stuff. Exercise stimulates the energy producers in our cells (the mitochondria) in both number and size, a phenomenon termed "mitochondrial biogenesis," which leads to greater energy production. In other words, including exercise as part of our lifestyle leads to more energy.

The list continues. Regular exercise boosts your endorphins, improving your mood and countering stress and anxiety. It builds your self-esteem (you're doing what you didn't think you could), your social life (you meet like-minded folks), and helps slow down aging (and I know of no one looking to speed that up).

Oh, did I mention it's also a great way to help lose weight? I said goodbye to a solid 30 pounds when I got off the couch and started running, and the weight loss itself boosted my energy level.

TRY THIS SHIFT

The exercise shift follows the same principle involved in improving your diet. If you can pinpoint and tackle your most common pitfalls, you better your odds. When it comes to exercise, the two most common pitfalls/excuses are:

➤ I'm too tired.

➤ I don't have enough time.

Starting small, and keeping it simple, bypasses both those pitfalls. Exercise is movement, and it can be incorporated in a myriad of ways. Setting the standards too high in the beginning is a rookie mistake. It is absurd to think most people will get off the couch and run ten miles with ease, and even if they did, it would not be sustainable on a regular basis.

Walking also is movement, and it represents a shift from a lifestyle centered on sitting down. This sedentary lifestyle tends to build a strong bond between the chair and our rear ends, and even if you live an active lifestyle outside your workday, sitting for hours is just not good for the human body long term.

Start Small

There are small and big ways to add more movement. A little Googling is sure to provide a long list. I've found, however, that a long list can become an excuse to do nothing at all, so I suggest picking a few and starting there. Some easy ways are:

> ➤ setting an hourly reminder to get up and walk around for a couple of minutes

> ➤ taking the stairs instead of the elevator

> ➤ a little less TV, a little more walking the dog

> ➤ a morning/evening walk

A few minutes a day, or even a few times a week, can start building a habit. Start small, then keep adding minutes in a gradual fashion until you reach a point of impact. That is my term for the feeling when you've done some activity, but not to the point you feel wiped out. Maybe that's 20 minutes a day for you, or maybe it's 60. Going for maximum each time may feel good a few times, but it can chip away at your motivation if it becomes your daily aim. If it's that difficult, you'll naturally start to avoid it, and a small amount of exercise is far better than none. Find a point that works for you, and you can always add on later.

Consistency + Accountability

After the small start, the next step to tackle is the challenge of consistency. What helps me is accountability. When I run, I run with a friend or a group. This means I have to show up, or risk the friendly but sincere wrath of my friends. For the gym, I take classes. It's much harder to quit and walk out amidst a group of people who've decided to stay.

Without accountability, I have a hard time staying consistent. Although I can occasionally rely on my willpower to carry me through, a regular dependence on willpower would be unrealistic. Classes also help me to keep things simple. I take classes at roughly the same times each week, so I can coordinate with my husband's and kids' schedules. The fewer barriers in my way, the easier it becomes to build this habit.

My goal here is not to give you a personalized plan, but to remind you that exercise provides benefits far beyond weight loss, no matter how the media focus upon slimming down as the objective. Exercise is a key ingredient in the chunky soup of physical and emotional factors that play a part in how we manage our energy, and how good we feel in life.

BENEFITS

Exercise:

> ➢ Helps manage weight

➤ Reduces risk of a lot of diseases/conditions (high blood pressure, high cholesterol, diabetes)

➤ Boosts your mood (combats depression, anxiety, makes you feel happier/more confident)

➤ Boosts energy (thus boosting many good things)

➤ Improves sleep

➤ Adds to your social life (other people exercise too)

➤ Can be fun (yes, really)

5

Self-talk + Self-definition

The thing always happens that you really believe in; and the belief in a thing makes it happen.
~ Frank Lloyd Wright, Architect, Writer

IN MY PRACTICE, I've seen 60-year-olds who can run circles around most 40-year-olds, 70-year-olds who couldn't care less what age means, and 80-year-olds who are going so strong it's as if no one told them they were supposed to slow down. I want their energy and enthusiasm when I grow up.

Whatever their constitution or circumstances, their attitude is a common theme–toward themselves as well as the world. It sets them apart. While they encounter obstacles like anyone else, they deal with them differently from most people. If you paid close attention, you'd notice in their stories how they didn't let their inner critics hold them back. That's why they have some of the most interesting, fun, and inspirational stories to tell. From beating cancer to dealing with the loss of loved ones, these folks have managed to get through some tough life situations. They know there are no guarantees in life, yet they've managed to find the energy to keep moving. When faced with self-doubt and uncertainty, they kept going.

In their stories, I see proof that you don't have to wait until a certain age to benefit from their advice; you can do it now. The inner critic is forever ready to keep you safe and comfortable, which is its job. And it's an important and necessary job—but if you let that voice rule, it will drain your enthusiasm and hold you back from trying new things or pursuing your ambitions.

The other trouble with the inner critic is that the voice inside your head has been a long-term tenant. It would be silly to ask it to pipe down, move to a smaller room, and speak only when spoken to. And if you try arguing with it, that's a physically and emotionally draining process without a resolution.

A better way, and the one I've been working on, is to start changing that inner language.

When faced with a challenge or a new idea, if your first thought is an automated, negative perspective, it's time to start tweaking. Unless you're a born optimist, rest assured this skill can be learned. The language you employ toward yourself has a big say in whether you stay put or move forward.

TRY THIS SHIFT

Since I discussed dealing with the inner critic in my previous book, *The Light Shift*, and because this impacts all of us every day, I'm sharing that shift here:

The next time your inner critic gets loud and bossy, change up your language. A few select words can get this habit--and the difference--started. Here are some examples:

Inner voice: I can't stand my co-worker, Debbie.

Better: Debbie and I don't see eye to eye in many situations.

Even better: I need to focus on my work, and not let negative thoughts take over.

Debbie may not change, but my job satisfaction might. When luck goes against me:

Inner voice: It's no use. Some people have all the luck. I'll never make it at this rate.

Better: I need to work hard, be smart and create my own luck. Luck doesn't last long without effort.

I control what I can, rather than worry about what I can't. When change is difficult:

Inner voice: I can't change. This is what I've believed in since I was a kid.

Better: If it's not working, not changing will cause more harm than good.

Even better: I see it's not working, so I need

to try something different. Who knows, it
may turn out better than I expected!

And with a better attitude, the chances of a better
outcome can only improve.

Dealing with the inner critic is not easy. Even the
best find it challenging, and knowing that fills me
with a sense of relief, because it means my own inner
critic is no more dominant than those of others. I can
deal with it by changing the language I use to talk to
myself.

Your aim is not to completely shut out the inner
voice of negativity. It's useful, necessary, and impossible to eradicate even if that were desirable. Your aim
is to make small tweaks so you can stand taller when
facing the critic, rather than blaming others or beating
yourself down with your negative thoughts. When the
inner critic sets the tone of your mind, you shrink
when what you really want is to expand. Changing
your language patterns liberates you to grow.

BENEFITS

➢ Less negativity/more positivity builds courage
  and confidence, and over time, resilience in
  the face of challenges.

➢ You shift to a better perspective, choosing to
  keep moving despite feeling fear.

➢ It positively affects self-worth, which boosts
  your personal energy.

6

The Story on Limited Thinking

*I'd finally come to understand what it had been: a yearning for a way
out, when actually what I had wanted to find was a way in.*
~ Cheryl Strayed, Author

THEY SAY FORTUNE favors the bold, yet few of
us feel fortune is referring to us. Bold? Not me!

As I get older and more intent on staying true to
myself, I have realized something. Before I add anything new—a change, a habit, a mindset—I have to
grapple with and toss out some old story to which
I've been clinging.

At some point, maybe you've thought you
couldn't do something. The reasons are plenty: not
good enough, not smart enough, not pretty enough,
not tall enough, too old/young, only for the special
people. It's easier to believe them than try to change.
It took me years to understand, believe, and eventually do something to change some of those stories. I'm
still working on some others.

As frustrating as frustration is, it is a fantastic trigger which leads to questioning why. An automated "I can't do this" is limited thinking. If I can't do something, I want to know why not, especially if I really want it. I consider just the awareness of the 'I can't' instinctive response a huge win.

TRY THIS SHIFT

Can't lose weight? Can't run a 5K? Can't go up to a stranger and start a conversation? In a world where most things are outside our control, we can own and change our stories. Open the door to the possibility, and ask yourself how.

A few suggestions on how to go about changing your story:

➢ In an unscientific study that I totally made up, 96.3% of the reasons why we say we can't do something are excuses, which are not reasons. Ask someone who has been successful at what you want to achieve.

➢ Instead of dwelling on why you can't do something, try asking yourself why not. This helps define your obstacles, perceived or real. Then ask yourself: how? Make a list of possible ways, even if they seem impossible or crazy.

➢ Think of someone in your network who has done this seemingly impossible thing, or Google to find examples online. Has a 60-

year-old ever started her first business? Has a physically challenged athlete ever competed in the Olympics? Has a family of four ever gone from too much debt to debt-free? If such or similar persons don't exist, you're off the hook, and you can keep spending energy telling yourself about limiting impossibilities rather than wonderful possibilities.

If it's been done before (although it need not have been), you too can do it. Change one small story, and the second change seems a tad more doable; then the third, fourth, fifth, and so on. Each time you make your story a little more possible, you reclaim the energy you were expending to hold so tightly onto your limits. On a deeper level, you begin to establish neural pathways that lead you away from thoughts of limitation, and more toward asking yourself how you can do a thing, rather than telling why you can't.

BENEFITS

Changing the story, i.e. breaking limited thinking patterns helps reduce the energy drain that comes from negative thoughts, fears of real or imagined dangers, and any limits which keep us feeling trapped. It also helps lay down new neural pathways so our brains learn to shift away from limiting thoughts, making less limited thinking patterns feel more natural.

7

Expand

Stop acting so small. You are the universe in ecstatic motion.
~ Rumi, Poet, Scholar, Mystic

WHERE ATTENTION GOES, energy flows.

When my son was four years old, he went through a little phase. Anytime he thought he was in trouble, his shoulders would droop; he'd clasp his hands together and hunch his back. He would literally try to curl into a ball while standing. It was weird to watch, and a tad dramatic for, say, not picking up his Legos, but that's how he rolled.

To be honest, I can't say I haven't felt the same urge after a particularly horrific day. This instinct to shrink in response to negativity is not abnormal, but I noticed that its shrinkage impact stuck with me. The longer I'd let those thoughts marinate, the more tightness would build, and lo and behold, here came the slump. However, I lacked my son's juvenile secret weapon: the ability to bounce back into his cheerful self in 30 seconds as if nothing had happened.

I hope to re-master that lost childhood skill one day. In the meantime, I keep practicing.

Enthusiasm is by nature expansive and contagious, widening your world. When you focus on negative thoughts, your enthusiasm shrinks. This corset of stress, anxiety, or hopelessness is emotional as well as physical. You feel overwhelmed, dwarfed by the size of your worries. This type of deflating, diminishing energy works against you. It is also deceptive, even sneakily self-harmful. It gives your mind the illusion of doing useful work, when all it's doing is giving you something to gnaw on, like a useless part-time job where no task gets completed.

The more momentum you allow negativity to gain, the more it drains and shrinks you. Those well-worn negative spirals get more comfortable with each smooth slide. When you disrupt them, they gain no comfort. As you feel a negativity cycle coming on, time is of the essence. The sooner you disrupt it, the faster it will lose steam.

Why be satisfied with merely disrupting the negative slide, though? It is more difficult to take the next step after disruption, and shift from negative to positive, but when you can do so, this shift gains power. Easier said than done, I know, but every practice needs a starting point.

The first disruption is simple: a few deep breaths, to loosen the tightness and its death grip on your thoughts. Then unclench your body and move. This opens the door to the second step: acknowledge the situation for what it is, think beyond the immediate problem, and turn your focus to a possible solution. As the focus shifts, the tightness eases and you begin to expand. It does not mean that you pretend there isn't a problem, but helps clear the mental fog that leaves you feeling hopeless in the face of the problem. It will allow you to acknowledge and accept it, which lets you begin to work on it.

The purpose of this shift is to transition you to the next step: taking action. If you're busy taking action, you're working on a solution, not dwelling on your problem. Now you have purpose, and the energy will follow.

This is one of the subtlest and most difficult shifts...for me, at least. If it's easier for you, then more power to you, because this one took me years to make progress. I now see that I resisted releasing my grip on the negative thoughts to which I was so accustomed. Even after conscious effort, even now, I still find it challenging to stand at the brink of negative spirals and not give in.

Where attention goes, energy flows.

TRY THIS SHIFT

The goal of this shift is to set the stage for a quicker and less painful transition from negative spirals to solving problems. If you find yourself in a negative funk, or want to get better at spotting one approaching, try to:

➢ Be mindful when thoughts turn negative; acknowledge and counter with positive ones.

➢ Imagine your anxiety and worry to be a child half your size, which creates distance and also "defines" your negative thoughts into a more addressable shape than the ambiguous fog that is their common state. Then soothe this child or give it a timeout (described more in detail in my book, *The Light Shift*).

➤ Focus on gratitude. Think: "Even in this situation, I'm grateful for _____."

➤ Get physical: a walk, a run, or a swim. Another option is meditation or deep breathing/stretching.

➤ Release: write down and give release to your thoughts.

➤ Take action. Think: "I know the problem sucks, but what are four or five ways I can resolve or manage it?" Act: pick a couple and do them.

Even if this approach doesn't provide a direct solution, it can help improve your perspective on the problem before it drains you mentally and emotionally. Minimizing this drain safeguards your energy reserves. Working toward a solution will expand them.

If you need any further incentive, ask yourself this: how has giving in to negativity worked out for you in the past?

BENEFITS

Aside from numerous health benefits such as better immunity, lower risk of heart disease, slowed aging, lower cholesterol, and many more, expanding is essential to healthy relationships and workplace success. I can't remember the last time I heard people rave about associating with a gloomy Gus.

It also improves resilience when life throws you a curve ball, as it often will.

8

Own Your State

If someone says you're weird, say Thank You.
~ Ellen DeGeneres, Comedian

WHEN I WAS in college, all-nighters before finals were practically a rite of passage. A few kids could roll up hung over from a wild night of partying and still manage a passing grade. I was not gifted with such talents. You can look at it this way: they knew what they could do, just as I knew what I could not do.

Fast-forward a few years, I have come to value the gift of sleep, and I'm not afraid to refuse a drink. I also prefer to come back from vacation a day early to recoup, and I have become relentless about my alone time. Call it getting older, adulting, boring, whatever; I call it self-discovery. It changes over time, and that's okay. Know what works for you and what doesn't, and own it.

Consider your own energy levels at various times. Energy levels ebb and flow. You can't always be "on" or you'll often burn out. There are times when you need to push through, and others when you just say no (or wish you had). Incorporating "off" times keeps the good, productive, positive energy in your life. This may sound insignificant, but just like a daily date with your favorite donut, when you're not looking, the scale tips to the other side pretty fast.

Energy also varies as you interact with the outside world, and it affects those interactions. Hence the terms 'introvert' and 'extrovert.' If you set aside the labels, it is simply about knowing what gets you going versus what doesn't. If being around people All. Day. Long. adds oomph to your engine, it's a sign you need to keep doing it. If you guard your alone time with mama-bear-like ferocity so you can gather the dregs of your sanity, then keep doing that.

When bumps on the road leave you rattled, consider the idea of less denial and more awareness, of checking in and assessing your situation. You are who you are, you are where you are. If you own your reality, you stop wasting energy resisting it.

TRY THIS SHIFT

If getting a handle on your personal energy level has baffled you or seemed out of reach, seek to be more observant about your state of energy. Start by paying attention to times when you feel your best and your worst. The goal isn't to have things in black and white in neat little boxes. It is to notice your patterns, work with them as often as possible, and optimize results. In other words, be more "you." For example:

➤ Are you a morning person? If so, and you

wait until day's end to do creative work, you will be doing it with a tired brain. Better to devote the earlier part of the day to write, design, or brainstorm ideas.

> You love connecting with people. Your social calendar is always packed because you say yes to every event. You need down time to recharge, but you fear you'll miss out (especially when they post those pictures!). Consider being more selective in your acceptances, and own your need to connect with yourself.

> Your schedule has been hectic and you're under a lot of stress. Your go-to unwinding methods are binge-watching TV or a (second) bottle of wine. Consider giving your body and mind a different mode of decompression by sleeping more or getting light exercise. Oodles of studies have shown that more sleep and more movement lead to stress relief. They also help you disconnect from the endless loop of what you need to do, or didn't. Negative thoughts and stress have a harder time fighting a rested brain.

> You schedule time to get work done. As you settle in, you open up your social network time sink of choice. Before you know it, it's been half an hour. When you next check the time, the clock shows that it's time for regret over a wasted opportunity. Social media are like bags of chips. If you don't want to eat the bag of chips, it's better not to buy any; telling

yourself to eat seven chips and close the bag is a talent few possess. Instead, disconnect from the Internet, delete your apps, use programs like Freedom to block distractions, or use the Pomodoro technique, where you set a timer and work for 25 minutes, then take a break for five, repeat.

Look at the tradeoffs between what you're doing now and making a change that suits your patterns. Although patterns can change over time, it's worth the effort to be aware of yours so you know what's currently working and what's not. That shows you where to start.

If you don't know and understand your own patterns, it becomes too easy to allow others' patterns to govern you. That can lead to you feeling like you're not doing enough, or are not keeping up with others you perceive to be more successful. I have to keep reminding myself what works for someone else won't necessarily work for me. Getting clarity on my own patterns gives me direction and a better chance to make progress, which in turn helps me waste less energy on feelings of discouragement.

BENEFITS

This shift helps you to identify what already works for you, then use it to generate momentum for a new habit or change you're trying to implement. The sooner you own your patterns, the less you get in your own way, the more energy you can use to do what matters to you.

9

Now, Change Your State

We have too many high sounding words, and too few actions that correspond with them.
~ Abigail Adams, Second First Lady of the United States

ONE OF ISAAC Newton's laws states that an object at rest tends to stay at rest, while an object in motion tends to stay in motion, unless acted upon by an unbalanced force. In the world of physics, this is referred to as *inertia*.

In my own world and everyday life, I've noticed how certain events trigger activity or inactivity. For example, when I plop down on the sofa at the end of the day, an hour or two can fly before I realize I haven't accomplished a single thing. Perhaps it's different for you, but my chores or errands just wait around for me to do them. When I don't, this means stress later on.

Since I know that my couch is adhesive, and will hold me there for a wasteful length of time, I have to account for the trigger. During evenings where I feel the pull of the couch, and have important things to do, I make myself decide: get up and get things done, go to bed, or else not venture into the land of the couch until I'm done with what's necessary. It's not a perfect system, but now there are more wins than losses. Sorry, not sorry, couch.

In theory, daily decisions need not be so regimented. With two children, a home lacking in self-completing chores, and two working parents, dropping the ball too often is a big drain on energy and a block party invitation for stress. When I need to be in motion, resting is too often not worth the tradeoff. I'd rather save that energy for a better purpose.

To increase energy, or at the very least to interrupt its decline, it helps to know your triggers. My couch is my Everest, yours might be different.

TRY THIS SHIFT

Identify your triggers, and start interrupting.

–Are you a daily participant in the post-work sofa plop? Try the 20-minute rule.

Here's the gist: for the first 20 minutes after you get home, set a new pattern rather than fall into an old one. If you're tired, nap. If you want to read or write, do so. If you seek calm, meditate. If you have kids, spend it with them.

–Are you dragging out of bed every morning, late, then rushing to work? Adjust your sleep routine.

If you are hitting the snooze button daily, you probably drag yourself out of bed. It's easiest to tackle by making changes the night before, such as heading to bed 30 minutes or an hour earlier. Get your clothes ready the night before. Plan out what you'll eat for breakfast, and what time you need to leave home so you're not frazzled. This is so simple and basic, but that's exactly why people underestimate its effectiveness.

–Do you find it difficult to work out consistently? Seek to change the state in which you find yourself when your workout-related consistency breaks down. Examples:

Make plans with a friend to meet at the gym or for a run (accountability). Pack your clothes the night before if it's after work, or lay them out if it's before (convenience). Sign up for a class rather than a solo workout (more accountability). Incorporate more walking in your day (much better for your back if you work mostly sitting down). Find what triggers the slacking off, and change that situation.

This applies to mental energy as well. If you're anxious, change your focus to taking action toward solving the problem. If you're feeling down or brooding, shift your mood by blasting your favorite song or watching a funny movie. The idea is to identify when and where you tend to get stuck, and to plan ahead for ways to change your state.

BENEFITS

This shift helps you be more self-aware by acknowledging that you have some set, predictable states. Knowing these, you identify your specific triggers so you can shift towards changing them. Taken together, these steps allow you to break down previous habits that may not be serving you well, and build new ones that do.

10

Honesty

I don't like work but I like what is in the work--the chance to find yourself.
~ Joseph Conrad, Writer

AS I DRAFTED this chapter, I had just finished reading Cheryl Strayed's book, *Wild*. The story centers around her three-month solo hike across the Pacific Coast Trail. To prepare for her trip, Cheryl packs everything she needs into a backpack as heavy as a Volkswagen Beetle. As she tells it, she could barely stand straight with it strapped to her back. I was impressed, because I breathe a sigh of relief when I put down my purse after walking with it for a few hours.

It got me thinking about life's burdens. Not all our burdens are physical. The masks we put on, the stories we believe, the lies we tell others as well as ourselves; each of these takes its emotional and mental toll. Often it's what we've been taught and it's what we know. *Not smart enough. I can't lose weight; it's too much work. It's too late to start now. I can't afford it. Why me?*

What if you took off the mask and looked the lies in the eye? What if you aligned your inner compass so that it reflected on your outer life?

That might be one of the hardest things anyone can do on the journey to grow as a person.

Because of the hard work it requires at the outset, embarking on a journey of honesty is counterintuitive in some ways. You might find the idea heavy, your own VW Beetle to carry. But I think we forget how much the stories that don't serve us anymore or the lies we keep believing weigh us down and hold us back. Instead of riding on the backs of our strengths, we strive to use our energy for carrying (and defending) our weaknesses. We struggle inside to find and love ourselves, but on the outside we pretend we have it all figured out. That dishonesty is a heavy burden to bear.

Real honesty is not for the faint of heart, but it's a necessary shift if we want to make our limited time more meaningful. It may be time to let that toxic relationship go, revisit a childhood passion, and stop trying to keep up our insides with other people's outsides. This might rub the people around you the wrong way, but it will lighten the load. The relief you feel after shedding that weight might surprise, strengthen, even delight you.

TRY THIS SHIFT

Like any journey, this one begins with a step. Unlike some journeys, this one is not linear. In this shift, identify some small thing you do that doesn't please you, or something you don't do that you would like to be doing, and change your answer.

Starting small in one area will give you the courage and momentum to start in others. I think the easiest place to start is saying no to things we don't like but do just to fit in ("sure, I'll have another drink") and saying yes to things others might not ("I want to train for a marathon").

Perhaps you might find it easier to start a different way, like starting a daily journal, or doing Morning Pages, as described by author and artist Julia Cameron. Morning pages are a time to put down on paper all your thoughts as you begin your day, which acts as a release, creates awareness, and frees your mind from chatter. Penn Jillette (magician of Penn & Teller fame) said that if he looked back in his journals and found he was still struggling with the same problems as he was six months or a year ago, he needed to change something. Journals can also be a safe place to shed layers you've put on over time, but don't feel ready to remove in front of an audience.

Honesty also comes into play when making decisions. From choosing what you like to read, to not buying stuff you don't really need or want, to speaking or writing or acting in a joyful way. It can be how you talk to your children or your parents, what you choose to wear, or how you express your creativity.

The intent is never to be honest at the cost of causing harm or forcing your truth onto anyone else, but to choose honesty in a manner that is still respectful in the face of disagreement. This is not always easy to do, which is why it's rarely an overnight success. Like any mountain, you climb it one step at a time.

The ripple effects of even small steps of honesty spark tiny bursts of liberation. And nothing boosts your confidence, energy, and enthusiasm like feeling liberated, especially if you did it yourself.

BENEFITS

Shifting to living and practicing more honesty helps build your self-confidence, mental toughness (you're working from your strengths), and your enthusiasm (you allow yourself to do more of what you want).

11

Remove Toxic People

Misery loves company and also recruits it.
~ Jon Acuff, Author

YEARS AGO, I was flipping at random through a magazine and came across an article on toxic behavior. I had never heard that term before. It described toxic behavior as something definable, recognizable, and with potential for a significant impact on life.

Toxic behaviors include constant complaining, gossip, lies, drama, the need to dominate/control, victim mentality, and perpetual doom and gloom. The more time you spend exposed to a person who exhibits such behaviors—whether it's a family member, a friend, or a coworker—the deeper the effect. Toxic people are vampiric.

Toxic behaviors or toxic relationships leave you emotionally depleted, feeling bad about yourself, or in some way feeling negative, less than you ought to be. As with most behaviors, there's a spectrum of toxicity. It ranges from the super subtle to you-can-see-it-a-mile-away extreme, from low grade to full blast.

Perhaps you know someone like that? I know I did.

If you've heard of a person described having a certain aura or that they emit a certain kind of energy, you understand. Interacting with toxic behavior feels like having the sunshine–and your energy–stolen from your life.

If you're not careful, time spent with toxic people will chip away at your dreams, your hopes, and your self-esteem. A combination of good intentions and strong resolve can only go so far. Life is too short to endure this pain. The less time they're in your world, the better. As much as you might want to 'fix' or 'cure' them, that is ultimately up to them, not you.

The most effective antidote I've found is to get smart about identifying them, then doing my best to deny them a valuable place in my life.

TRY THIS SHIFT

Identify the energy vampires in your life. How?

Simple: take note of how you feel after you've spent time with the people you most often see. Bearing in mind that a single bad day does not a toxic person make, you can get a fair sense of the uppers and the downers. The ones that leave you feeling up are the ones you keep. The ones that leave you feeling drained, low, or bad about yourself should get less space in your life. But what if it's someone you can't realistically avoid? If you have to work on a project with complaining Suzy from Accounting, you can't just stop showing up. If critical Joe is your supervisor, you definitely can't stop showing up. In order to keep your job, you need an alternative to not showing up. What if it's your sibling, or your next-door neighbor? When that's the case, be it family, friend or frenemy, you can try to:

➤ minimize how much you interact with the person

➤ say no as often as possible to social situations

➤ keep conversations brief, limit engagement

➤ change the subject of conversation if the person gets too intense

The last two work really well when gossip and drama threaten to pick up steam. Knowing what you're dealing with can help you disconnect, distance yourself from them, and get to a place where you can interact without taking the same harm you once did. Overall, the lower the frequency of interaction, the better.

In his book *Do Over*, Jon Acuff talks about dealing with difficult coworkers: "If one of your co-workers is difficult to work with but they treat everyone the same way, they're not your foe. They're your annoyance. Welcome to the planet. Some people are annoying."

The decision to identify toxic persons may sound judgmental, but it's not. It's an acknowledgement that such people are not the right fit for you; your energies are just not compatible. Knowing that, you can modify your interaction with them. Perhaps their energies are compatible with someone else's, but that's outside your concern. Only they can determine their own relationships.

On the flip side, be aware of your own energy. If you yourself partake in negative behaviors, remember that energy is contagious by type. Let your own good energy through, and it will attract more of the same. Negative energy will do likewise.

BENEFITS

➤ Reducing the value you grant to toxic behavior.

➤ Reduces leaks from your energy bucket.

➤ Distances you from relationships that serve neither side.

➤ Creates space to attract more positive energy into your life.

12

First Simplify, Then Simplify 2.0

Practice yourself for heaven's sake, in little things; and thence proceed to greater.
~ Epictetus, Greek Stoic Philosopher

EVER SINCE MARIE was a little girl, she'd had a passion for keeping things organized. She might even say she was a little obsessed. Years later, which included formal training in and more obsessing about organization, Marie became a best-selling author. Her consulting business had a waiting list, and *Time* magazine listed her as one of the world's 100 most influential people.

This is how Marie Kondo inspired over 2 million people to pick up her book, *The Life Changing Magic of Tidying Up*. Including me.

If two million people are interested in decluttering and organizing their homes, having too much stuff is a fairly common issue. Agree or disagree with Marie's methods, I have yet to hear anyone who carried through with simplifying and then complained about having more space, less clutter, and less stuff to keep up with. I have, however, heard that less stuff helped them feel less stressed and more at peace.

I'd venture to guess that decluttering frees up their mental energy and puts them in a more positive frame of mind. I'll add here that I gave Marie's methods a fair shot, and I can honestly say I haven't missed any of the items I gave away. So let's take the principle a step further: how about if we declutter a few more things...say, your to-do list?

Maybe everything you think needs to get done...doesn't.

Whether using Marie's methods or your own, it makes sense to get rid of what's not essential before organizing, checking off, or fretting over.

Simplify 2.0

Once you're on your way to declutter and decrease, the next level of simplifying rides on the coattails of the first and makes it more effective. Simplifying 2.0 is about simplifying the decision-making process, especially those you make on a regular basis.

Steve Jobs had his signature look of black turtleneck and blue jeans, Mark Zuckerberg must have a gazillion grey t-shirts, and designer Tom Ford is almost always in black and white. You and I may not travel in the same circles, but there's no reason we can't steal the idea, and not just for wardrobe. When you consider the sheer number of decisions you make on an average day, it takes energy to approach the usual ones as if for the first time. Some of them don't merit that level of attention. Those first-time feelings, the newness, and the discovery may give you a better payoff in your romantic life, not in making the precise best choice of what you eat for breakfast each morning.

You can pare down such decisions by having a set go-to system for the smaller or routine things, making for a smoother day. Such as:

> ➤ Do you travel a lot? Simplify and automate your travel bag. Have the essentials ready to go, including a few of your preferred items of clothing.

> ➤ Do you eat breakfast every day? Stock up on your daily items so you don't have to decide what to eat in the morning.

> ➤ Do you head to the gym in the mornings? Have your gym bag packed and ready to go.

> ➤ Stressed out deciding what to wear to work? Have a few outfits that you can mix/match/repeat, at least until you find a better method that works for you.

> ➤ Have too much on your schedule? If you are spread too thin, it's time to look at what you can say no to without compromising your priorities. Look at your to-do list and ask yourself, "Do I really need to do this, or am I doing it because it's the way I've always done it?"

As the number of decisions you make in a day

multiplies like Kardashian stories in the media, you may find yourself drained by day's end. At that point, the only attractive options might be getting some shut-eye, or watching mindless TV. If you needed to make fewer decisions, you might feel less drained. Simplifying can streamline both your living environment and the seemingly perpetual decision-making process, letting you shift your energy to more meaningful parts of your day. Would you rather be making small decisions than learning a new skill, exploring a hobby, or reading that hot new thriller you've been looking forward to?

One objection that might come to mind: doesn't automating decisions clash with one's creative side, creating boredom? Not in my view. If the simplifying 2.0 process leaves you feeling that way, I'd consider it a sign that your system needs fine tuning. As with any shift, you must adapt it to your life. For example, if choosing clothes feels fun and creative for you, then maybe it's one of the good parts of your life, and needs to stay.

Whether you've got a company to run, kids to raise, or a side business to start, removing the non-essentials and simplifying the daily basics can deter the drain from your daily energy reservoir.

TRY THIS SHIFT

Start with the morning, or whenever your day begins:

> ➤ Clothing: If you don't have a designated uni-form, you get to design your own. Get a few combos together and try this out for a week,

be it business suits, workout gear, or outfits for chauffeuring kids all day. If simplicity is your thing, black and white are a good (and classic) place to start.

➤ Morning routine: Take an honest look at how your mornings usually go. Again, a week is a good timeframe to start refining. Maybe a green smoothie and a run every day gets your engines running. Mine is coffee, toast, and writing. Whatever your best wake-up activity is, put it on automatic.

➤ Eating: No, going to the same fast food place doesn't count; let's pick something healthier. Rich Roll, the ultra Ironman/marathon runner, prefers a big salad for lunch every day. Even if you don't plan to train like he does; you could automate differently. You could stock your car or office with almonds, apples, or bananas for go-to snacks so you don't give in to the junk foods.

I've found that if you look hard enough, there are plenty of ways to simplify. When you set systems of your choosing, not only does it take some daily decisions off your plate, it helps maintain consistency for habits you're trying to build. It's no secret that new habits like going to the gym, writing, or eating better don't happen overnight, so automating parts of these activities can increase not only your energy reserves, but also your chances of success.

BENEFITS

This shift helps you by:

➤ Reducing minor, regular decision-making so you can shift that energy to more meaningful choices and actions.

➤ Helping you build consistency as you sustain a new habit.

➤ Reducing stress.

13

Creativity, Where Are You Now?

I want to sing like the birds sing, not worrying about who hears or what they think.
~ Rumi, Poet, Scholar, Mystic

REMEMBER BACK IN kindergarten, when you got crayons and paper, and the teacher turned you loose to create? Do those days seem a lifetime ago?

Creativity may be one of the most important skills to rediscover in today's world. Although we got an early start with our finger paints and crayons, we got lost on our way to adulthood. Many of us stopped embracing creativity, and decided we lacked any. If you, like me, had given in to the inner critic saying "I'm not creative" or "I wasn't born with creative skills," it's time to tune out that voice. Most people think of creativity as just another division of haves and have-nots, something done as a matter of course in kindergarten but which going forward is only for the special, gifted few.

On the contrary, creativity is a skill we can all cultivate.

In her book *The Gifts of Imperfection*, discussing her findings on whole-hearted living, author and researcher Brené Brown makes three statements:

➤ There's no such thing as creative people and non-creative people. There are only people who use their creativity and people who don't.

➤ The only unique contribution that we will ever make in this world will be born of our creativity.

➤ If we want to make meaning, we need to make art.

Why creativity? Because creative pursuits make life interesting and more fulfilling. They lead to innovation and problem-solving. And when we are interested and more fulfilled, guess what we have more of? Energy.

Creativity is not limited to what we consider "the arts." Some may say: "I don't have time to be creative; I have real responsibilities." They're incorrect, because creativity is a valuable skill in any arena, be it running a household or leading a team. Creative ideas that solve problems or fulfill desires lead to new businesses, bigger promotions, and tastier tacos. If your creative ideas add value, it increases demand for your skills. A greater embrace of your own creativity is key to doing an outstanding job at those real responsibilities, with the added benefits of satisfaction and enthusiasm.

Creativity fuels enthusiasm and joy, and pushes us to stretch our mental muscle and look at challenges in ways we may not have previously. Creativity brought us the wheel, smart phones, and everything in between. It is also a release, an avenue to vent frustration and allow ourselves space to do things we've always wanted, or to try something new.

The problem is, the encouragement to be creative all but disappears past childhood. Unless you grew up with a family member or friend who understood the value of creativity, it probably gave way to the overshadowing responsibilities of life. To bridge that gap later in life will take some effort, but it can also be a lot of fun. To stretch your creative muscle, you have to give yourself permission to do it and be intentional about making time for it.

When that muscle starts working, and you find yourself enjoying it–even if it's the little stuff–you know you're on to something good.

TRY THIS SHIFT

To encourage more creativity in your life, here are a few suggestions to set the stage:

➢ Make the time. For many of us, if we don't schedule it, it won't happen. Pick a time in the next couple of weeks and block it off on your calendar.

➢ Start small. Don't feel pressured to dedicate a whole day or have a finished product right away.

➤ Be positive. Don't start with the mindset that it's a waste of time. Grant your productivity hat a short break. even if at first you begrudge that break.

The field of options is huge, so pick whatever pulls you toward it. Try "artistic" activities–color, paint, draw, design, cook, make videos–anything that piques your interest. It can be as simple as a grown-up coloring book or taking a salsa class, or it could be embarking on a bigger venture, like starting an organic garden or restoring a classic car. If you have kids, they are less removed from the creative encouragement days; they can be the pros you learn from, as well as your handy minions.

As the gates creak open, you might start to see how creativity has a place at work as well; it's just never been presented as such.

One activity that encourages the creative habit and deserves special mention is from author, investor, and chess master James Altucher, who is a big advocate of writing down ten ideas a day. He credits this practice of stretching his mental muscle with helping him reinvent his career and go from broke to rich multiple times. Writing down ten ideas a day on different topics can put you on the path to becoming an idea machine.

BENEFITS

Opening avenues of creativity helps reduce stress, anxiety, depression, and negative emotions. It also encourages a greater sense of well-being, resilience, and personal growth. And did I mention it can be really, really fun?

14

Resistance

If you take risks and face your fate with dignity, there is nothing you can do that makes you small; if you don't take risks, there is nothing you can do that makes you grand, nothing.
~ Nassim Nicholas Taleb, Essayist, Statistician, Risk Analyst

IF YOU HAVEN'T read Steven Pressfield's book, *The War of Art*, I recommend it. He dissects the concept of Resistance, an internal force that stands between the life we live and the unlived life within us. More specifically, Pressfield defines Resistance as that which shows up when we attempt "any act that rejects immediate gratification in favor of long-term growth, health, or integrity."

Whether you want to...

 ➢ start a new habit (exercise, more sleep, less stress),

> ➤ pursue a dream (play guitar, travel the world),

> ➤ break an old habit (smoking, sugar),

> ➤ start a business (serve others, make money),

… or follow any aspiration that could make your life better, you will have to contend with the force of Resistance.

Resistance shows up in the form of negative emotions: unhappiness, procrastination, boredom, dissatisfaction, and the like. Its goal is to win. Resistance wins by preventing you from starting. Once you get going, it fights you every step of the way, then tries to prevent you from finishing. Its primary weapon is fear.

So what does this have to do with energy?

If Resistance wins, dreams are laid by the wayside, fear takes over, and the growth and transformation you're looking for doesn't happen. Do you ever spend mental or emotional energy wishing your dreams would come true?

Resistance - 1, Enthusiasm for life - 0.

No amount of coffee or Red Bull is going to reverse that.

Like any fear, Resistance is persistent. The good news is that there's something you can do about it.

TRY THIS SHIFT

Since Mr. Pressfield has already figured out how to deal with Resistance, I will relay a few of his techniques here. Whether you're trying to lose weight,

build a meditation practice, start a new business project, or whatever your goal or dream:

> Be patient. Accept delayed gratification, know that things worth having often take time and persistence.

> Seek order. Reduce chaos, have a system or a plan (an imperfect one beats none at all).

> Demystify. Avoid getting caught in the idea of something; focus instead on doing the work that will take you closer to it.

> Act in the face of fear. Everyone experiences fear, but only taking action despite that fear will make any real impact.

> Accept no excuses. Too busy? Too old/young? Not smart enough? These are excuses we've all used at some point. It's time to call them what they are and keep moving.

BENEFITS

Acknowledging and tackling Resistance helps you move past paralysis and start taking steps toward what you want. It helps you take the energy you spend on fear and channel it toward what grows and fulfills your life. While there are no guarantees, proceeding despite fear increases chances of getting real results.

15

Your Insides versus Their Outsides

You act like mortals in all that you fear, and like immortals in all you desire.
~ Seneca, Stoic philosopher

WE WANT MANY things: good health, love, financial freedom, friends, accomplishment, career success, and more. As we strive to achieve these, there are bound to be moments of discouragement, when things don't go like we hoped. Others succeed when we do not. When we're down, we tend to kick ourselves.

One very painful form of self-kicking is to begin comparing yourself to those who seem to be doing better than you. Soon, you feel unworthy, not good enough, or that F-word: "failure." In fact, several F-words come to mind.

Never in human history has it been so easy to contract comparisonitis. Thanks to the Internet, it's at our fingertips. The Internet is our sixth sense, a way to see others' highlights, then use them as weapons of self-sabotage. The always-on, always-connected phenomenon blurs the fact that each of us is on a different journey, which is easy to forget when we're busy looking at other people's lives and not feeling so hot about our own. If you tune in at your most discouraged and vulnerable state, the negative thoughts and emotions tend to spill forth.

This negativity is a mental energy drain, making things harder on yourself than they have to be. If you do not observe this happening, or if you see but disregard it, the negativity can leave you emotionally crushed.

This comparison of apples to watermelons, of our private lives to others' public personas, of inner sensitivities to the outer world, is unfair to say the least. We know this, yet we still do it. When cruising our social media feeds in that state of mind, it takes but a moment to feel deflated. And because it happens so smoothly and effortlessly, it's not until you're licking your wounds that you start to wonder, 'how the heck did I get here?' And all you did was use your fingertips.

If your mood and energy are flagging to begin with, or you're making efforts to shift up, be aware of how your online interactions affect you. If they roll off your back, no worries. If you know you're vulnerable, better to step away.

TRY THIS SHIFT

If scrolling on social media and watching your connections posting pictures from the best vacation ever, winning yet another award, or partying it up with twenty of their best friends leaves you feeling negative or bad about yourself, take note. Then step away, or risk feeling flat and depleted.

While I've alluded primarily to online interactions, the same applies to real-life interactions. Those energy drainers were with us before the Internet, and they have not gone away. Minimize your real time with them, just as you minimize your online time perusing their lives' contrast with your own.

Better yet, choose a replacement activity with the goal to get yourself into a better, energized state. It should uplift and comfort you. Consider spending time with people who love and support you, watching a funny movie, getting a good night's sleep, or blasting your favorite music. Physical exercise can also work wonders, and gets your endorphins pumping. One of the best ways I've found of getting out of a funk is to speed up my transition from dwelling on negative thought by doing something, no matter how small, about the source of frustration. I grant that it's difficult to do most times, but it is the path out of frustration.

Like most shifts, the progress at the time seems miniscule. I only did one small thing! However, if I look back over the years of doing this, I have made significant progress. My brain is less resistant to the idea of taking action, and the negative thoughts loosen their grip. It is a practice, and because negative thoughts are bound to surface, it is a practice well worth your while.

BENEFITS

This shift reminds you to be more aware of what you allow in your life when in a fragile state, and to take firmer control of it. This helps conserve the energy you need to recover and rise back up toward strength and purpose.

16

A Conflict of Energy

Champions keep playing until they get it right.
~ Billie Jean King
Former World No.1 professional tennis player

IF TELEVISION HAS taught me anything, it's that I'm just not producing the level of drama required for a hit reality show. That is the price I pay for striving to have a peaceful life, or choosing alternative ways to add adventure and excitement.

When you have to deal with someone you don't like, or someone who forcefully disagrees with you, how does it usually go? Do you stay calm with a smile on your face, elated about the impending discourse? Or do you often feel a smidge of tension, a slight tightening in your insides, or, if it's a not-so-minor disagreement, do you get angry, frustrated, and upset? Most people make wide detours around conflict because it's uncomfortable and a huge source of stress.

Chances are you deal with several daily minor

conflicts, rather than multiple all-out, MMA-style blowouts. Like the snarky coworker who constantly interrupts you, rude drivers on your commute, or poor customer service. How to respond?

Depending on the type of conflict, your response may be to avoid it or resolve it, one way or another. Whatever your handling of a given conflict, it helps to be aware of the way your handling affects you. Is winning at all costs worth the stress? How about when you compromise, or walk away all together; how does that impact you? Do you prefer to resolve things at the outset, before they've had time to pick up steam, or keep delaying until the situation mushrooms?

In my earlier, more naive years, I made some poor hiring decisions in my business, and let things go further than I should have before dealing with them. Looking back, while avoiding letting those employees go, I spent a lot of needless energy fretting. I felt extremely uncomfortable at the thought of firing someone, something I had never done before. Not only did that cost me money and energy, it affected other members of my team and hurt my business. Eventually, I hired outside help to get my business back in shape, and the first step was to get the right team on board.

I learned my lessons. I had to:

➢ know how conflict affects me;

➢ address it early before it snowballs;

➢ handle it myself or get help.

TRY THIS SHIFT

Pay attention to how you deal with conflict. (Notice how so many things we want in life start with knowing our own selves better?) What's the source? What are your options? Blaming others may feel good in the short term, but is rarely the right solution. Read up, get help, or hire help.

That pesky co-worker? How about some headphones to indicate that you're busy? Or a quick conversation letting him/her know you're swamped.

Road rage is a daily conflict for many. Try leaving a few minutes earlier, since rage is quicker to rise when you're in a rush. Or perhaps try a different route. Turn up the music, or listen to podcasts on subjects that interest you. The latter have improved my commutes to the point that I now look forward to them.

Dealing with poor customer service is tricky, but it's a fact of life. I find being extra-extra-nice gives me unexpected wins, and in other cases, you just live to try another day.

Some conflicts are not even worth dealing with, given the big picture, and so not worth the stress they might appear to entail. While this process may not address 100% of conflicts you encounter, if it helps address even some of them, even in a small way, that is still a shift forward.

As you start to diffuse even the minor conflicts, you'll find yourself less susceptible to your usual triggers, which will lower the stress dial just a notch. This helps conserve your mental and emotional energy.

BENEFITS

Knowing your triggers as well as your comfort level when faced with daily conflicts can help you deal with them proactively, which lowers your stress level and prevents leaks from your finite reservoir of mental and emotional energy.

17

Shift It Forward

I found myself praying: "May I love and accept myself just as I am."
~ Tara Brach, Author of Radical Acceptance

WHEN MY FIRST book came out in paperback, I decided to throw a little party to celebrate. I was nervous, not being too comfortable with an "all about me" theme. I was also scared, wondering if anyone would show up, so I asked a friend to help me put it together. I hoped the free wine and food would be enough of an incentive. Thanks to my friend (and the wine), people did show up. That's when I met Kevin.

Kevin came as a guest of another friend, didn't know anything about me or my book, but stood first in line to get a copy and a picture. We eventually became friends.

A couple of weeks later, while I was having a really crappy day, I received a message from Kevin. He said he was trying to eat better, and because of something he'd read in my book, he was able to skip eating donuts at work. He was super excited about it. He said he walked right by them, and called it a win.

Some people in this world are saving lives in the jungle or making prosthetic limbs for the physically disabled. I helped someone skip a donut.

As trivial as that was, his message made me smile. It became the highlight of my day, which had been horrible up to that point. Kevin didn't know it, but he ended up helping me. I felt better, and suddenly things weren't as bad as they seemed.

We don't always get validation after helping someone, but performing the act itself has its own way of shifting your own internal energy. It gives you all the feels, as they say.

If we pay attention, there are plenty of opportunities throughout the day for these small, helpful acts. An added bonus is that they distract us from our own troubles swirling around in our head, often snapping us out of a negative funk. Sometimes, that's all it takes to muster up the energy to keep moving forward, even if it's for just one more day.

TRY THIS SHIFT

The hardest yet best time to reach out and help someone is when you're the most frustrated with your own problems. I'm not referring to major life events, such as the loss of a loved one, losing a job, serious illness, etc., but to the daily frustrations that constantly nag at us and sap our willpower and energy.

The next best time is anytime.

If you are on the lookout, you will notice the opportunities. Maybe you see the chance to reach out to a friend going through a rough time, or offer to run an errand for an elderly neighbor. Sometimes it's just being present, and paying attention to the person in front of you. In an age of a million distractions, being present in the moment is no small feat.

I recently heard this question, and now I try to ask it of my kids as often as I can: "Who did you help today?" It's a great alternative to and has a better response rate than "How was school today?" I can't ask it of my children without asking it of myself: "Who can I help today?"

BENEFITS

This shift gives you energy by distracting you from your own problems, and gets you out of your own head. Chances are you just might learn something, feel good, deepen a friendship, and get back on track.

Doing (More of) What You Desire

THE HUMAN MIND is truly miraculous and never will you see it spring more beautifully into vigorous action than when you want it to change.

Misery is comfortable, which is why so many prefer it.

Happiness requires courage. And effort.

Effort requires energy.

There's a lot of talk about doing what you love, finding your passion, about chasing your dream.

Fulfilling your deepest desires...who wouldn't want that? If you look past the long line of people waiting to make your dreams come true for the low, low price of just $997, the idea sounds magical.

In that teeny tiny space between this magical idea and the often-instinctive dismissal, there lies the possibility of fulfilling your desires.

The catch is that the price tag is a question mark, and the only person who can make that sale is you.

Unfulfilled desires lead even the most talented to a stall, the most successful to boredom, and can leave any of us disinterested and stuck. In other words, miserable.

If there's something you love, there's something you can do about it, however small.

If you want to find your passion, you can start by exploring what you're passionate about.

If you want to chase your dream, your job doesn't have to be the reason you can't start working on it.

Surrendering to your desires means doing more of what pulls you. The energy you spend pushing away will be better spent fueling what you want in a more excited state of mind, otherwise known as enthusiasm.

Enthusiasm is the magical force that gives you the energy to keep moving forward, try new things, make life more interesting. It's also what helps you stay the course when things don't go as planned and you have to deal with obstacles. When faced with tasks that are necessary but not fun, enthusiasm helps get the job done.

Seem too difficult? When my inner voice starts spouting that at me, I remind it that the alternative is staying where I am, dealing with boredom, dissatisfaction, and staying stuck for the foreseeable future. If I had let my inner critic win, I'd never have run a business, run a marathon, or written a book, or made any of the changes, large or small, that have created ripples in all facets of my life.

Once you open that door, you'll find your enthusiasm automatically rise up, and you'll find the energy to shift forward.

Acknowledgements

To my husband, Venu Rao, and my kids, for making this all possible.

To my editor, J.K. Kelley, I'm so glad you helped me steer this ship. I'm so grateful.

To Joel, thank you for your cover art and your friendship.

To Jill, Sue, Trang, Henrik and Maria, for your endless kindness, support and wisdom.

About the Author

RITU RAO is a dentist and writer. Whether running an ultramarathon or her own business, she condenses others' wisdom and her own to spread her message: small steps are the key to personal change. She is also the author of *The Light Shift: 21 Simple Ways to Make Your Days Interesting, Get Unstuck and Beat the Daily Grind.* She lives in Dallas, Texas with her husband and two children.

Notes

Notes

Notes

Notes

Notes